Bảo Anh Lạc Bookshelf 65

# THE GREAT PARINIRVANA CEREMONY

Composed
by
**Bhikṣuṇī TN Giới Hương**

Hong Duc Publishing

**HUONG SEN BUDDHIST TEMPLE**
19865 Seaton Avenue
Perris, CA 92570, USA
Tel: 951-657-7272, Cell: 951-616-8620
Email: huongsentemple@gmail.com
thichnugioihuong@yahoo.com
https://www.facebook.com/Huong.Sen.Riverside
Web: www.huongsentemple.com


ISBN: 978-1-0881-0176-6

# THE FIRST WORDS

Every day Nuns and Buddhists at Hương Sen Buddhist Temple, California, USA, have practiced and recited following the Vietnamese scripture, "Nghi Lễ Hàng Ngày – 50 Kinh Tụng và các Lễ Vía trong Năm" (Daily Chanting – Fifty Discourses and Annual Festivals) of the Pureland Sect, which was composed in 2021 by Bhikkhunī Thích Nữ Giới Hương. It is based on the original ritual of her late Master, the Venerable Elder Hải Triều Âm at Liên Hoa Temple and Dược Sư Temple.[1]

Since many Vietnamese-Americans, Hispanic, native Americans, and English speakers have come to Huong Sen Temple in search of practice and ritual, Bhikkhunī Giới Hương composed an English version of **DAILY MONASTIC CHANTING**. It encompasses 16 popular rituals to serve the spiritual needs of any Buddhist sect, including the Pure Land and Meditation Traditions as below:

1. Practice Meditation
2. The Ceremony for Peace
3. The Rice Offering to Buddhas
4. The Lunch Offering at the Dining Hall
5. The Ritual Offering Food To Hungry Ghosts
6. The Pureland Course of Amitabha Sutra
7. The Medicine Buddha Sutra
8. The New Year Ceremony

1 Please read: http://www.huongsentemple.com/index.php/vn/phat-phap/kinh-ta-ng-ca-a-cha-a-hs/6256-nghi-le-hang-ngay-20.

9. The Great Parinirvana Ceremony
10. The Buddha's Birthday Ceremony
11. The Ullambana Festival (Parents' Day)
12. The Marriage Ceremony
13. The Blessing Ceremony for The Deceased
14. The Ancestral Ceremony
15. The Enlightened Buddha Ceremony
16. The Uposatha Ceremony (Reciting Precepts)

With regard to mindful chanting, we take sources from the sacred book, Chanting from the Heart: Buddhist Ceremonies and Daily Practices of Thích Nhất Hạnh. In the field of the Pureland School, we have taken material from the above Vietnamese scripture, "Nghi Lễ Hàng Ngày," and translated it into English.

We should chant at least once a week, any place and any time, or more often if we have more time. The chant will help to avoid negative thoughts, defilements, distractions -any of the myriad things that intrude into the one-pointed mind. We definitely feel the connectedness with Dharma (the Buddha's teaching), we feel the spirit being lifted up, the awakening and the settling of the mind to enter meditation. We will become bright, enduring, detached, diligent, generous, loving, understanding and so on . . . because we practice following the chanting and the role model of Buddhas.

Chanting out loud or silently listening to chanting can also be very relaxing as we go about our day. It can be used to calm our mind before work or sleeping.

For the sake of all the general practitioners, there are some changes, combinations, additions, reductions, and creations made in this English version. This is the first time that both traditions have been combined in an English version for the necessary needs at Huong Sen Buddhist Temple.

We would like to gratefully acknowledge with special thanks the Buddhas, Boddhisattvas, Sanghas, the English translators, Master Thích Nhất Hạnh, our Late Respectful Teacher - Venerable Elder Bhikkhunī Hải Triều Âm and others. You all provided us the awakening words to remind and guide us in the right way of practice. We will keep chanting, learning and practicing it until we and all beings get the enlightenment as well as realize our Buddha nature.

If there is any merit in compiling this book, may it be shared with all sentient beings. May they diligently practice and soon gain the way of love and understanding.

Reciting the sutras, practicing the way of awareness
gives rise to benefits without limit.
We vow to share the fruits with all beings.
We vow to offer tribute to parents, teachers, friends,
and numerous beings who
give guidance and support along the path.
(Thích Nhất Hạnh)

Hương Sen Temple, Riverside, California

March 15, 2023

**Bhikkhunī TN Giới Hương**

# THE GREAT PARINIRVANA CEREMONY

At the full moon of the second month in lunar year, the Buddha Entering Nirvana Ceremony is often organized. Buddhist disciples perform this ritual do memorial or honor the great enlightened life of Sakyamuni Buddha and his last period of entering the Parinirvana.

1. Introduction
2. The incense offering
3. Salutation
    3.1. Gratitude the Buddhas and Bodhisattvas
    3.2. Gratitude the Buddhas in the past
    3.3. Gratitude the Arahats
    3.4. Gratitude the Ancestors
4. The Repentance Gatha
5. Opening verse
6. Chanting the Great Parinirvana Discourse
7. The insight that brings us to the other shore
8. Read the Names of the Buddhas and Bodhisattvas
9. May the day and the night be well

10. The four collections
11. Prayer
12. Salutation thousands of Buddhas in three times
13. Taking refuge at three jewels
14. Sharing the merit & verse for closing
15. The divine gatha.

***

## 1. INTRODUCTORY

Leader: **Today is the full moon day of the second month, we are** (the leading Bhikkhuni...) **and the sangha gathered at the main hall of... to present the flowers, incense, cake, fruit and conduct the ritual to celebrate the Day Sakyamuni Buddha entering the Parinirvana.**

**We remembered after getting the enlightenment, out of compassion, the Shakyamuni Buddha travelled here and there to delivery Dharma for the sake of many. He was a human being just as we are, but His understanding and love were developed to a very high degree, and he became a fully awakened being. He shared his knowledge from his enlightened experience in order that people can live mindfully, awakenly and liberatedly.**

**Today at the ceremony, we do memorial or honor the event the Buddha passed away under the Sala trees at Kushinagar, India; we promise to follow the Budda's way to return our Precept-meditation-wisdom and Buddha nature. We will spread Dharma - the global message of the happiness and liberation to pay the gratitude to the Buddha.**

**May the Buddha-Dharma-Sangha be presented everywhere in order that people can nurture the Buddha-seeds and transform the greed, anger, and delusion to be the love, understand and toleration.**

**May all sentient and non-sentient beings soon attain the Buddhahood as the Shakyamuni Buddha did.**

**May all beings are always the bodhi awaken friends and protect the Three Jewels in the world forever.**

**Namo Shakyamuni Buddha.** (3 times) (ooo)

## 2. THE INCENSE OFFERING

Leader: **In gratitude, we offer this incense to all Buddhas and Bodhisattvas throughout space and time.**

**May it be fragrant as Earth herself, reflecting our**

**careful efforts, our wholehearted mindfulness, and the fruit of understanding, slowly ripening.**

**May we and all beings be companions of Buddhas and Bodhisattvas.**

**May we awaken from forgetfulness and realize our true home.** (o)

**Namo Offering the Incense**
**Bodhisattva Mahasattvas.** (3 times) (ooo)

## 3. SALUTATION IN GRATITUDE

(All Sangha members read)

### 3. 1. GRATITUDE THE BUDDHAS AND BODHISATTVAS

1. **Offering light in the Ten Directions, the Buddha, the Dharma, and the Sangha, to whom we bow in gratitude.** (o) (1 prostration)
2. **Teaching and living the way of awareness in the very midst of suffering and confusion, Shakyamuni Buddha, the Fully Enlightened One, to whom we bow in gratitude.** (o) (1 prostration)
3. **Cutting through ignorance, awakening our hearts and our minds, Manjushri, the Bodhisattva of Great Understanding, to whom we bow in gratitude.** (o) (1 prostration)
4. **Working mindfully, working joyfully for**

**the sake of all beings, Samantabhadra, the Bodhisattva of Great Action, to whom we bow in gratitude.** (o) (1 prostration)

5. **Seed of awakening and loving kindness in children and all beings, Maitreya, the Buddha to-be-born, to whom we bow in gratitude.** (o) (1 prostration)
6. **SeeingtheBuddhaineveryone,Sadaparibhuta, the Bodhisattva of Constant Respect, to whom we bow in gratitude.** (o) (1 prostration)
7. **Showing the way fearlessly and compassionately, the stream of all our Ancestral Teachers, to whom we bow in gratitude.** (ooo) (1 prostration)

## 3.2. GRATITUDE THE BUDDHAS IN THE PAST

1. **The Buddha Vipashyin, to whom we bow in gratitude.** (o) (1 prostration)
2. **The Buddha Shikhin, to whom we bow in gratitude.** (o) (1 prostration) **The Buddha Vishvabhu, to whom we bow in gratitude.** (o) (1 prostration)
3. **The Buddha Krakkucchandha, to whom we bow in gratitude.** (o) (1 prostration)
4. **The Buddha Konagamana, to whom we bow in gratitude.** (o) (1 prostration)

5. **The Buddha Kashyapa, to whom we bow in gratitude.** (o) (1 prostration)
6. **The Buddha Shakyamuni, to whom we bow in gratitude.** (o) (1 prostration)
7. **The Bodhisattva of Great Understanding, Manjushri, to whom we bow in gratitude.** (o) (1 prostration)
8. **The Bodhisattva of Great Action, Samantabhadra, to whom we bow in gratitude.** (o) (1 prostration)
9. **The Bodhisattva of Great Compassion, Avalokiteshvara, to whom we bow in gratitude.** (ooo) (1 prostration)
10. **The Bodhisattva of the Great Vow, Kshitigarbha, to whom we bow in gratitude.** (ooo) (1 prostration)

### 3.3. GRATITUDE THE ARAHATS

1. **The Venerable Kashyapa, to whom we bow in gratitude.** (o) (1 prostration)
2. **The Venerable Shariputra, to whom we bow in gratitude.** (o) (1 prostration)
3. **The Venerable Maudgalyayana, to whom we bow in gratitude.** (o) (1 prostration)
4. **The Venerable Upali, to whom we bow in gratitude.** (o) (1 prostration)

5. **The Venerable Ananda, to whom we bow in gratitude.** (ooo) (1 prostration)

## 3. 4. GRATITUDE THE ANCESTORS

1. **Mother of Buddhas, Bodhisattvas, and all beings, nourishing, holding, and healing all, Bodhisattva Gaia, Great Mother Earth, precious jewel of the cosmos, to whom we bow in gratitude.** (o) (1 prostration)
2. **Radiating light in all directions, source of life on Earth, Mahavairocana Tathagata, Great Father Sun, Buddha of infinite light and life, to whom we bow in gratitude.** (o) (1 prostration)
3. **Seed of awakening and loving kindness in children and all beings, Maitreya, the Buddha to-be-born, to whom we bow in gratitude.** (o) (1 prostration)
4. **Showing the way fearlessly and compassionately, the stream of all our Ancestral Teachers, to whom we bow in gratitude.** (ooo) (1 prostration)

# 4. THE REPENTANCE GATHA

**All wrongdoing arises from the mind.**

**When the mind is purified, what trace of wrong**

**is left?**

**After repentance, my heart is light like the white clouds that have always floated over the ancient forest in freedom.** (o)

**Namo the Repentance**
**Bodhisattva Mahasattvas.** (3 times) (ooo)

## 5. OPENING VERSE

**The Dharma is deep and lovely.**

**We now have a chance to see, study, and practice it.**

**We vow to realize its true meaning.**

**Namo Shakyamunaye Buddhaya.** (3 times) (ooo)

## 6.CHANTING THE GREAT PARINIRVANA DISCOURSE

(Translated into English by Charles Patton)

**Thus have I heard. One time the Buddha was staying at the city of Kusinagara, the birthplace of the great worthy, on the shore of the Ajiravati River between a pair of Sala trees. At that time, the World Honored One was accompanied by a great bhiksu congregation numbering eighty nayutas of kotis of people, encircling him front and back. On the fifteenth day of the second month, the time of his entry into Nirvana was**

**eminent.**

**World Honored One, Now wishes to enter Nirvana.**

**All that is born in the world**
**Will return to death.**
**While their life spans may be measureless**
**It is necessary that they have an end.**
**The sage, too, must have his waning.**
**What comes together and assembles must break apart And so the healthy years eventually come to a end.** (o)

**The prosperous form is transgressed by disease**
**And life is swallowed up by death.**
**There is nothing (no dharma) that lasts forever.**
**The power of the Kings who have attained sovereignty,**
**Who have no comparison,**
**They all pass on and perish.**
**[My] life span is also so.**
**The myriad sufferings turn without end**
**Flowing round without cease or respite.** (o)

**The three realms are all impermanent**
**And all existences are unhappy.**
**What has paths, roots, natures, and signs**
**All these are empty and non-existent.**
**Such destructible things (dharmas) flow round**

**Always having sorrow, anxiety,**
**Fear, and advancing evils.**
**Old age, disease, and death are the decline into distress.**
**These are without bounds**
**That are transgressed by change, destruction, and bitterness.**
**The afflictions that are the bondages**
**Are just like the silkworm's cocoon.**
**Why would anyone with wisdom**
**Be happy in this place?**
**This body is a collection of sorrows**
**All of which are impure.**
**Stopping the bonds and tumors**
**The roots of which are without righteousness or blessing.**
**Going up to the heavenly body**
**Is also so.** (o)

**The desires are all impermanent**
**And that is why I do not covet attachments.**
**Departing from desires, skillfully contemplating [things], And realizing the true Dharma:**
**This is the ultimate cutting off of existence.**
**Today I shall go into Nirvana,**
**Crossing over to that other shore**
**And leaving behind all of the suffering.**
**This is why on this day**

**You should only feel a marvelous happiness."**

**We now shall see the Buddha's Nirvana.**
**We who have destroyed the ocean of miseries**
**Are now saddened and grieved**
**As though losing our own mothers.**
**Poverity-stricken and without aid or protection are we,**
**Just like a weary and ill person who,**
**Without a healer, follows his own mind**
**And eats what he should not eat.** (o)

**The sentient beings are afflicted with diseases,**
**Constantly are they looking after injuries.**
**Far removed are they from the Dharma and medicine king,**
**They imbibe and consume incorrect and harmful medicines.**
**This is why the Buddha, the World Honored One,**
**Should not leave us behind.**
**Like a country without a lord,**
**The people of which are stricken with famine,**
**We are also so.**
**Losing your aid and the flavor of the Dharma.**
**Now we hear of the Buddha's Nirvana.**
**Our minds are perplexed and disordered.**
**Like that great earthquake,**
**Confused and mistaken are we in the our ways.**

**When the great Sage enters Nirvana**
**The Buddha-sun shall set upon the land.**
**The Dharma waters will all dry up**
**And we shall surely die.** (o)

**The Tathagata's parinirvana**
**Is to the sentient beings who are most distressed**
**Just like an elder's son**
**Who recently attended his mother and father's funeral.**
**How can we on this day**
**Not be apprehensive?**
**The Tathagata going and leaving us**
**Is just like casting away tears.**
**The Tathagata entering Nirvana**
**Is like one who will not return.** (o)

**We and the sentient beings**
**All will be without any aid or protection.**
**With the Tathagata entering Nirvana,**
**Even the animals**
**Are all anxious and fearful.**
**Distressed and pained are their thoughts.**
**Just like when the sun when it first rises**
**It's light is a brilliant ray blazing**
**And when it is about to return its radiance**
**Again dies and all is darkened,**
**The Tathagata's spiritual power is a light**

**That can remove our distress.** (o)

**It is just as when the sun goes behind a mist and becomes completely hidden. This great Nirvana that is a subtle and wondrous Sutra is also again so, being produced in the world. If there are sentient beings who have an ear for the Sutra, they would be capable of putting to rest all evils and not longer be amidst wicked karma.** (o)

**This great Nirvana is profound and deep, its perspective inconceivable. Skillfully speaking of the nature of the Tathaagata is subtle and esoteric. What does this mean? Good sons and good daughters should regarding the Tathagata bring forth the thought of his being constantly abiding, devoid of any change, the true Dharma that is unending, and the sangha imperishable. This is why one should cultivate numerous skillful means and endevour to study this text. It would not be long for such a person to attain the supremely unexcelled enlightenment. This is why this Sutra is called the completion of infinite virtue. It is also called the enlightenment that is invulnerable. Because it is invulnerable is the reason that it has obtained the title 'Great Parinirvana'. Because it possesses the good light, is it like the summer days. Because the body is limitless, it is called the Great Nirvana.** (o)

**Namo Shakyamunaye Buddhaya.** (3 times) (ooo)

# 7. THE INSIGHT THAT BRINGS US TO THE OTHER SHORE

**The Heart of Prajnaparamita (Perfect Wisdom)**

**Avalokiteshvara while practicing deeply with the Insight that Brings Us to the Other Shore, suddenly discovered that all of the five Skandhas are equally empty, and with this realization he overcame all Ill-being (suffering).** (o)

**Listen Sariputra, this Body itself is Emptiness and Emptiness itself is this Body. This Body is not other than Emptiness and Emptiness is not other than this Body. The same is true of Feelings, Perceptions, Mental Formations, and Consciousness.** (o) **Listen Sariputra, all phenomena bear the mark of Emptiness; their true nature is the nature of neither Birth nor Death, neither Being nor Non-being, neither Defilement nor Purity, neither Increasing nor Decreasing.** (o)

**That is why in Emptiness, Body, Feelings, Perceptions, Mental Formations and Consciousness are not separate self-entities. The Eighteen Realms of Phenomena which are**

**the six Sense Organs, six Sense Objects, and six Consciousnesses are also not separate self-entities.** (o)

**The Twelve Links of Interdependent Arising and their Extinction are also not separate self-entities. Ill-being, the Causes of Ill-being, the End of Ill-being, the Path, insight and attainment, are also not separate self-entities. Whoever can see this no longer needs anything to attain.** (o)

**Bodhisattvas who practice the Insight that Brings Us to the Other Shore see no more obstacles in their mind, and because there are no more obstacles in their mind, they can overcome all fear, destroy all wrong perceptions and realize Perfect Nirvana.**

**All Buddhas in the past, present and future by practicing the Insight that Brings Us to the Other Shore, are all capable of attaining Authentic and Perfect Enlightenment.** (o)

**Therefore, Sariputra, it should be known that the Insight that Brings Us to the Other Shore is a Great Mantra, the most illuminating mantra, the highest mantra, a mantra beyond compare, the True Wisdom that has the power to put an end to**

**all kinds of suffering.** (o)

**Therefore, let us proclaim a mantra. To praise the Insight that Brings Us to the Other Shore. Gone, gone, gone beyond, gone to the other shore, awake, rejoice!** (3 times) (o)

**Namo the Great Compassionate Avalokiteshvara Bodhisattva.** (3 times) (ooo)

## 8. MAY THE DAY & NIGHT BE WELL

**May the day be well and the night be well.**
**May the midday hour bring happiness too.**
**In every minute and every second, may the day and night be well.**
**By the blessing of the Triple Gem, may all things be protected and safe.**
**May all beings born in each of the four ways live in a land of purity.**
**May all in the Three Realms be born upon Lotus Thrones.**
**May countless wandering souls realize the three virtuous positions of the Bodhisattva Path.**
**May all living beings, with grace and ease, fulfill the Bodhisattva Stages.**
**The countenance of the World-Honored One, like the full moon**
**or like the orb of the sun, shines with the light**

**of clarity.**
**A halo of wisdom spreads in every direction, enveloping all with love and compassion, joy and equanimity.**

**Namo Shakyamunaye Buddhaya.** (3 times) (ooo)

## 9. READ THE NAMES OF BUDDHAS & BODHISATTVAS

**The river of attachment is ten thousand miles long.**
**The waves on the ocean of confusion stretch so far.**
**If you wish to go beyond the realms of samsara,**
**Recollect the Buddha with one pointed mind.** (o)

**The Pure Land is available in our True Mind.**
**Amitabha manifests from the true nature of things,**
**Shining light on the three worlds and the ten directions,**
**Always abiding in the present moment.**
**May I go back to Amitabha Buddha,**
**The founder of the Pure Land,**
**The source of limitless lifespan.**
**May I with one heart visualize and recollect this holy name.**

**Namo Shakyamunaye Buddhaya, the Fully Enlightened One.** (3 times) (o)

**Namo Amitabhaya Buddhaya, the Buddha of Infinite Light.** (3 times) (o)
**Namo Manjushri, the Bodhisattva of Great Understanding.** (3 times) (o)
**Namo Samantabhadra, the Bodhisattva of Great Action.** (3 times) (o)

**Namo Avalokiteshvara, the Bodhisattva of Great Compassion.** (3 times) (o)

**Namo Kshitigarbhaya Bodhisattvaya, the Bodhisattva of Great Aspiration.** (3 times) (ooo)

## 10. THE FOUR RECOLLECTIONS

**The Blessed One is worthy and fully self-awakened. I bow before the Buddha.** (o)

**The teaching is well expounded by the Blessed One. I pay homage to the Dharma.** (o)

**The community of the Blessed One's disciples has practiced well. I pay respect to the Sangha.** (o)

**The Noble Teacher in whom I take refuge**

**is the One who embodies and reveals the Ultimate Reality, is the One who is worthy of all respect and offering,**

**is the One who is endowed with perfected**

**wisdom,**

**is the One who is endowed with right understanding and compassionate ac- tion,**

**is the One who happily crossed to the shore of freedom, is the One who looked deeply to know the world well, is the highest charioteer, training humankind,**

**teaching gods and humans,**

**the Awakened One, the World-Honored One.** (o)

**The Teaching given by my Noble Teacher**

**is the path I undertake, the teaching well-proclaimed,**

**is the teaching that can be realized right here and right now, is the teaching that is immediately useful and effective,**

**is the teaching inviting all to come and see directly,**

**is the teaching that is leading to the good, the true, the beautiful,**

**extinguishing the fire of afflictions;**

**it is a teaching for all sensible people to realize for themselves.** (o)

**Practicing the teachings, the Noble Community in which I take refuge is the community**

**that goes in the direction of goodness, in the direction of truth,**

**in the direction of beauty, in the direction of righteousness;**

**is the community that is composed of four pairs and eight kinds of holy people; is the community that is worthy of offerings, worthy of great respect, worthy of admiration, worthy of salutation;**

**is the community standing upon the highest fields of merit in all of the world.** (o)

**The Mindfulness Trainings, the wholesome way of living taught by my Noble Teacher, is the wonderful practice that remains unbroken,**

**that remains harmonious, that remains flawless, that remains refined; is the wonderful practice that has the capacity to prevent wrongdoing and to prevent danger;**

**is the wonderful practice that has the capacity to protect self and others and to reveal beauty; is the wonderful practice that is leading to concentration, leading to peacefulness, leading to insight, leading to non-fear; is the wonderful practice that shows us the way to total emancipation and long-lasting happiness.** (o)

**Namo Shakyamunaye Buddhaya.** (3 times) (ooo)

## 11. PRAYER

**Today is the full moon day of the second month in lunar year, we are** (the leading Bhikkhuni...) **and the sangha gathered at the main hall of... to organize the Sakyamubi Buddha Enlightened Day. We sicerely offer the flowers, incense, cake and fruit to the Buddha, conduct the chanting the Enlightened Search Sutta and the Greater Discourse to Saccaka, practiced meditation, and the meritorious deeds.** (o)

**We would like to return this merit to pray the Buddhist (the full name, the Dharma name, old), together with the householders and all Sangha members present here are always healthy, happy and live for long. May all year round be auspicious and joy. May our bodhicitta firm; our wills are steady; and we will gain self-awareness as well as the perfective enlightenment.** (o)

**Again, we give back this merit to for the deceased...** (the full name, the Dharma name, longevity…) **with our ancestors and parents in the past, the heroic warriors sacrificed for the country, the deceased died in rivers, accidents and other reasons. There**

are twelve kinds of souls with names or unname. May all of them overcome the suffering ocean of the bad karma and be peaceful at the Pure land and practice with Buddhas and Bodhisattvas.

Finally, may all sentient beings soon complete the Way of Love and Understanding.

Namo Amitabha Buddhaya. (ooo)

## 12. SALUTATION THOUSANDS BUDDHAS IN THREE TIMES

There are many the great causes

The ten directions, three lives and realms

I keep my body and mind pure

Pay homage at all without being left behind. (o)

We pay respects sincerely to the four graces of the three realms:

Namo the Buddhas of the kalpa thousands in the past. (o) (1 prostration)

Namo the Buddhas of the kalpa thousands in the present. (o) (1 prostration)

Namo the Buddhas of the kalpa thousands in the future. (o) (1 prostration)

# 13. TAKING REFUGE AT THREE JEWELS

**-I take refuge in the Buddha,**
**the one who shows me the way in this life.**
**I take refuge in the Dharma,**
**the way of understanding and of love.**
**I take refuge in the Sangha,**
**the community that lives in harmony and awareness.** (o) (1 prostration)

**-Dwelling in the refuge of Buddha,**
**I clearly see the path of light and beauty in the world.**
**Dwelling in the refuge of Dharma,**
**I learn to open many doors on the path of transformation.**
**Dwelling in the refuge of Sangha,**
**shining light that supports me, keeping my practice free of obstruction.** (o) (1 prostration)

**-Taking refuge in the Buddha in myself,**
**I aspire to help all people recognize their own awakened nature,**
**realizing the Mind of Love.**
**Taking refuge in the Dharma in myself,**
**I aspire to help all people fully master the ways of practice**
**and walk together on the path of liberation.**

**Taking refuge in the Sangha in myself,**
**I aspire to help all people build Fourfold Communities,**
**to embrace all beings and support their transformation.** (ooo) (1 prostration)

## 14. SHARING THE MERIT & VERSE FOR CLOSING

**Reciting the sutras, practicing the way of awareness gives rise to benefits without limit.**
**We vow to share the fruits with all beings.**
**We vow to offer tribute to parents, teachers, friends, and numerous beings who give guidance and support along the path.** (o)

**May we be born now in the Pure Land**
**within the heart of a lotus flower.**
**In the moment when the lotus blooms,**
**we touch the reality of no-birth and no-dying.**
**May Buddhas and Bodhisattvas be our companions**
**on the wonderful path of practice.** (o)

**May we end all afflictions**
**so that understanding can arise,**
**the obstacles of unwholesome acts be dissolved,**

**and the fruit of awakening be fully realized.** (o)

**Namo Amitabha Buddhaya.** (ooo)

## 15. THE DIVINE GATHA

**Gods, nagas, asuras and yakshas**
**Come here, with all your heart listen to the Dharma.**
**Protect the Buddha-dharma so that it may endure**
**And all may act in the spirit of the Buddha's teaching.**
**When you have come to hear the Dharma,**
**Whether you are under the earth or in the sky,**
**Look at all beings with the eyes of love.**
**Day and night abide in the right practice.**
**May the world always be safe and secure,**
**Impregnated by the merit of wisdom and love.**
**May all the obstacles of wrong doing be dissolved.**
**May we live behind afflictions**
**and know always how to touch peace and joy.**
**May the Sangha with determination observe the precepts,**
**Be diligent in the practice of meditative concentration.**
**May the flower of awakened understanding**

**bloom beautifully**
**And everywhere may all species have happiness.**

**Namo the Dharma Protective**
**Bodhisattva Mahasattva.** (3 times) (ooo)

# BẢO ANH LẠC BOOKSHELF

## Dr. Bhikṣuṇī TN Giới Hương composed

### A. THE VIETNAMESE BOOKS

1. *Bồ-tát và Tánh Không Trong Kinh Tạng Pali và Đại Thừa* (Boddhisattva and Sunyata in the Early and Developed Buddhist Traditions).
2. *Ban Mai Xứ Ấn* (The Dawn in India), (3 tập).
3. *Vườn Nai – Chiếc Nôi* (Phật Giáo Deer Park–The Cradle of Buddhism).
4. *Quy Y Tam Bảo và Năm Giới* (Take Refuge in Three Gems and Keep the Five Precepts).
5. *Vòng Luân Hồi* (The Cycle of Life).
6. *Hoa Tuyết Milwaukee* (Snowflake in Milwaukee).
7. *Luân Hồi trong Lăng Kính Lăng Nghiêm* (The Rebirth in *Śūrangama* Sūtra).
8. *Nghi Thức Hộ Niệm, Cầu Siêu* (The Ritual for the Deceased).
9. *Quan Âm Quảng Trần* (The Commentary of Avalokiteśvara Bodhisattva).
10. *Nữ Tu và Tù Nhân Hoa Kỳ* (A Nun and American Inmates).
11. *Nếp Sống Tỉnh Thức của Đức Đạt Lai Lạt Ma Thứ XIV* (The Awakened Mind of the 14th Dalai Lama).
12. *A-Hàm: Mưa pháp chuyển hóa phiền não* (*Agama – A Dharma Rain transforms the Defilement*), 2 tập.
13. *Góp Từng Hạt Nắng Perris* (Collection of Sunlight in

Perris).

14. *Pháp Ngữ của Kinh Kim Cang* (The Key Words of Vajracchedikā-Prajñāpāramitā-Sūtra).
15. *Tập Thơ Nhạc Nắng Lăng Nghiêm* (Songs and Poems of Śūraṅgama Sunlight).
16. *Nét Bút Bên Song Cửa* (Reflections at the Temple Window).
17. *Máy Nghe MP3 Hương Sen* (Hương Sen Digital Mp3 Radio Speaker): Các Bài Giảng, Sách, Bài viết và Thơ Nhạc của Thích Nữ Giới Hương (383/201 bài).
18. *DVD Giới Thiệu về Chùa Hương Sen*, USA (Introduction on Huong Sen Temple).
19. *Ni Giới Việt Nam Hoằng Pháp tại Hoa Kỳ* (Sharing the Dharma - Vietnamese Buddhist Nuns in the United States).
20. *Tuyển Tập 40 Năm Tu Học & Hoằng Pháp của Ni sư Giới Hương* (Forty Years in the Dharma: A Life of Study and Service—Venerable Bhikkhuni Giới Hương), Thích Nữ Viên Quang, TN Viên Nhuận, TN Viên Tiến, and TN Viên Khuông.
21. *Tập Thơ Nhạc Lối Về Sen Nở (Songs and Poems of Lotus Blooming on the Way).*
22. *Nghi Thức Công Phu Khuya – Thần Chú Thủ Lăng Nghiêm* (Śūraṅgama Mantra).
23. *Nghi Thức Cầu An – Kinh Phổ Môn* (The Universal Door Sūtra).
24. *Nghi Thức Cầu An – Kinh Dược Sư* (The Medicine Buddha Sūtra).

25. *Nghi Thức Sám Hối Hồng Danh* (The Sūtra of Confession at many Buddha Titles).
26. *Nghi Thức Công Phu Chiều – Mông Sơn Thí Thực* (The Ritual Donating Food to Hungry Ghosts).
27. *Khóa Tịnh Độ – Kinh A Di Đà* (The Amitabha Buddha Sūtra).
28. *Nghi Thức Cúng Linh và Cầu Siêu* (The Rite for Deceased and Funeral Home).
29. *Nghi Lễ Hàng Ngày - 50 Kinh Tụng và các Lễ Vía trong Năm* (The Daily Chanting Rituals and Annual Ceremonies).
30. *Hương Đạo Trong Đời 2022* (Tuyển tập 60 Bài Thi trong Cuộc Thi Viết Văn Ứng Dụng Phật Pháp 2022 - A Collection of Writings on the Practicing of Buddhism in Daily Life in the Writing Contest 2022).
31. *Hương Pháp 2022* (Tuyển Tập Các Bài Thi Trúng Giải Cuộc Thi Viết Văn Ứng Dụng Phật Pháp 2022 - A Collection of the Winning Writings on the Practicing of Buddhism in Daily Life in the Writing Contest 2022).
32. *Giới Hương - Thơm Ngược Gió Ngàn*, Nguyên Hà.
33. *Pháp Ngữ Kinh Hoa Nghiêm* (2 tập). Thích Nữ Giới Hương.
34. *Tinh Hoa Kinh Hoa Nghiêm*. Thích Nữ Giới Hương. NXB Hương Sen.
35. *Phật Giáo và Đại Dịch Coronavirus Covid-19*. Thích Nữ Giới Hương.
36. *Phật Giáo – Tầm Nhìn Lịch Sử Và Thực Hành.* Hiệu đính: Thích Hạnh Chánh và Thích Nữ Giới Hương.

## B. THE ENGLISH BOOKS

1. Boddhisattva and Sunyata in the Early and Developed Buddhist Traditions.
2. *Rebirth Views in the Śūraṅgama Sūtra.*
3. *Commentary of Avalokiteśvara Bodhisattva.*
4. *The Key Words in Vajracchedikā Sūtra.*
5. *Sārnātha-The Cradle of Buddhism in the Archeological View.*
6. *Take Refuge in the Three Gems and Keep the Five Precepts.*
7. *Cycle of Life.*
8. *Forty Years in the Dharma: A Life of Study and Service—Venerable Bhikkhuni Giới Hương.*
9. *Sharing the Dharma -Vietnamese Buddhist Nuns in the United States.*
10. *A Vietnamese Buddhist Nun and American Inmates.*
11. *Daily Monastic Chanting.*
12. *Weekly Buddhist Discourse Chanting.*
13. *Practice Meditation and Pure Land.*
14. *The Ceremony for Peace.*
15. *The Lunch Offering Ritual.*
16. *The Ritual Offering Food to Hungry Ghosts.*
17. *The Pureland Course of Amitabha Sutra.*
18. *The Medicine Buddha Sutra.*
19. *The New Year Ceremony.*
20. *The Great Parinirvana Ceremony.*

21. *The Buddha's Birthday Ceremony.*
22. *The Ullambana Festival (Parents' Day).*
23. *The Marriage Ceremony.*
24. *The Blessing Ceremony for The Deceased.*
25. *The Ceremony Praising Ancestral Masters.*
26. *The Enlightened Buddha Ceremony.*
27. *The Uposatha Ceremony (Reciting Precepts).*
28. *Buddhism: A Historical and Practical Vision.* Edited by Ven. Dr. Thich Hanh Chanh and Ven. Dr. Bhikṣuṇī TN Gioi Huong.
29. *Contribution of Buddhism For World Peace & Social Harmony.* Edited by Ven. Dr. Buddha Priya Mahathero and Ven. Dr. Bhikṣuṇī TN Gioi Huong.
30. *Global Spread of Buddhism with Special Reference to Sri Lanka.* Buddhist Studies Seminar in Kandy University. Edited by Dr. Ven. Kahawatte Siri Sumedha Thero and Dr. Bhikṣuṇī TN Gioi Huong.
31. *Buddhism In Sri Lanka During The Period of 19th to 21st Centuries.* Buddhist Studies Seminar in Colombo. Edited by Prof. Ven. Medagama Nandawansa and Dr. Bhikṣuṇī TN Gioi Huong.

## C. THE BILINGUAL BOOKS (VIETNAMESE-ENGLISH)

1. *Bản Tin Hương Sen: Xuân, Phật Đản, Vu Lan (*Hương Sen Newsletter: Spring, Buddha Birthday and Vu Lan, annual/ Mỗi Năm).
2. *Danh Ngôn Nuôi Dưỡng Nhân Cách - Good Sentences*

*Nurture a Good Manner.*

3. *Văn Hóa Đặc Sắc của Nước Nhật Bản-Exploring the Unique Culture of Japan.*
4. *Sống An Lạc dù Đời không Đẹp như Mơ - Live Peacefully though Life is not Beautiful as a Dream.*
5. *Hãy Nói Lời Yêu Thương-Words of Love and Understanding.*
6. *Văn Hóa Cổ Kim qua Hành Hương Chiêm Bái -The Ancient- Present Culture in Pilgrim.*
7. *Nghệ Thuật Biết Sống - Art of Living.*

## D. THE TRANSLATED BOOKS

1. *Xá Lợi Của Đức Phật* (Relics of the Buddha), Tham Weng Yew.
2. *Sen Nở Nơi Chốn Tử Tù* (Lotus in Prison), many authors.
3. *Chùa Việt Nam Hải Ngoại* (Overseas Vietnamese Buddhist Temples).
4. *Việt Nam Danh Lam Cổ Tự* (The Famous Ancient Buddhist Temples in Vietnam).
5. *Hương Sen, Thơ và Nhạc* – (Lotus Fragrance, Poem and Music).
6. *Phật Giáo-Một Bậc Đạo Sư, Nhiều Truyền Thống* (Buddhism: One Teacher – Many Traditions), Đức Đạt Lai Lạt Ma 14th & Ni Sư Thubten Chodren.
7. *Cách Chuẩn Bị Chết và Giúp Người Sắp Chết-Quan Điểm Phật Giáo* (Preparing for Death and Helping the Dying – A Buddhist Perspective).

# BUDDHIST MUSIC ALBUMS

## from POEMS of THÍCH NỮ GIỚI HƯƠNG

1. *Đào Xuân Lộng Ý Kinh* (The Buddha's Teachings Reflected in Cherry Flowers).
2. *Niềm Tin Tam Bảo* (Trust in the Three Gems).
3. *Trăng Tròn Nghìn Năm Đón Chờ Ai* (Who Is the Full Moon Waiting for for Over a Thousand Years?).
4. *Ánh Trăng Phật Pháp (*Moonlight of Dharma-Buddha).
5. *Bình Minh Tỉnh Thức* (Awakened Mind at the Dawn) (*Piano Variations for Meditation*).
6. *Tiếng Hát Già Lam* (Song from Temple).
7. *Cảnh Đẹp Chùa Xưa* (The Magnificent, Ancient Buddhist Temple).
8. Karaoke *Hoa Ưu Đàm Đã Nở* (An Udumbara Flower Is Blooming).
9. *Hương Sen Ca* (Hương Sen's Songs).
10. *Về Chùa Vui Tu* (Happily Go to Temple for Spiritual Practices).
11. *Gọi Nắng Xuân Về* (Call the Spring Sunlight).
12. *Đệ Tử Phật* (The Buddha's Disciples).

*Please consult the **Bảo Anh Lạc Bookshelf** at this website:*

*http://huongsentemple.com/index.php/en/about-us/b-o-anh-l-c-bookshelf*

**THE GREAT PARINIRVANA CEREMONY**

Author: Bao Anh Lac Bookshelf 65 - Huong Sen Buddhist Temple

HONG DUC PUBLISHING

Tel.: 024.39260024 - Fax : 024.39260031

Email: nhanxuatbanhongduc65@gmail.com

Responsible for publishing

Manager: **Bui Viet Bac**

Responsible for the content

Editor in Chief: **Ly Ba Toan**

Editor: **Phan Thi Ngoc Minh**

Presenter: **Vu Dinh Trong**

Editing the copy: **Vu Dinh Trong**

*Printing quantity: 1,000 copies, Size: 14.5 x 20.5 cm*

*Printed at: Tram Anh Printing,*

*159/57 Bach Dang, Ward 2, Tan Binh District, HCM City.*

*Registration number: 3209-2023/CXBIPH/29-92/HĐ*

*ISBN: 978-604-434-657-1*

*Publishing decision: 321/QD-NXBHD dated September 29, 2023*

*Finished printing and deposit in the third quarter of 2023*

www.ingramcontent.com/pod-product-compliance
Lightning Source LLC
LaVergne TN
LVHW022325200926
848481LV00004B/1431